DESERT

TREK

COLLINS

ISBN 0-00-196134-9
Copyright © 1989 Victoria
House Limited.
All rights reserved.
First published in the UK
by William Collins Sons and
Company Ltd, 8 Grafton
Street, London W1X 3LA.
Printed in the UK.

DESERT TREK

Written by Prof. C. Milner
and A. Langley
Illustrated by Paul Johnson
Edited by Moira Butterfield

Contents

DESERT PROFILE

There are deserts in Africa, Asia, Australia, South America and North America. In fact nearly a fifth of the Earth's land surface is desert, where less than 25cm of rain falls each year. In most deserts the temperature is hot during the day and much colder at night.

Most people imagine sand dunes when they think of deserts; but there are also stony, salty, mountainous and flat deserts.

Some deserts are dry because they are far away from the sea. They get none of the moisture which sea winds normally carry over land. Other areas are dry because they are in the shadow of a mountain range.

When clouds pass over high mountains they drop all the moisture they contain, so the land on the other side of the range gets no rain at all.

The Sahara is the World's hottest and largest desert. It stretches across North Africa, covering an enormous area almost as big as the USA.

Nowadays, people cross the Sahara by car, but it is still an exciting and dangerous journey, when you could encounter fierce sandstorms and dangerous creatures. You can find out more about desert dangers like this on p.12.

Most of the centre of Australia is desert plain, called 'the Outback'. It is dotted with large rocky outcrops such as Ayres Rock, famous for its Aborigine paintings.

Like most deserts the Outback is rich in wildlife. It is home to amazing creatures such as the kangaroo, the thorny dragon and the ostrich. You can find out more about desert animals on p.14.

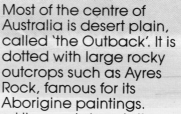

In North American desert areas there are some fascinating animals and plants to be seen. For instance, you might come across a 15m high cactus (see p.20), the strange tracks of a 'sidewinding' snake (see p.16) or hear the deadly sound of the diamond backed rattlesnake (see p.12).

There are many smaller World deserts. They include the Gobi desert in Mongolia, the Atacama desert in Chile, the Kalahari in Southern Africa and the desolate Arabian desert, first crossed by Wilfred Thesiger in 1946. You can find out more about Thesiger and other desert explorers on p.6.

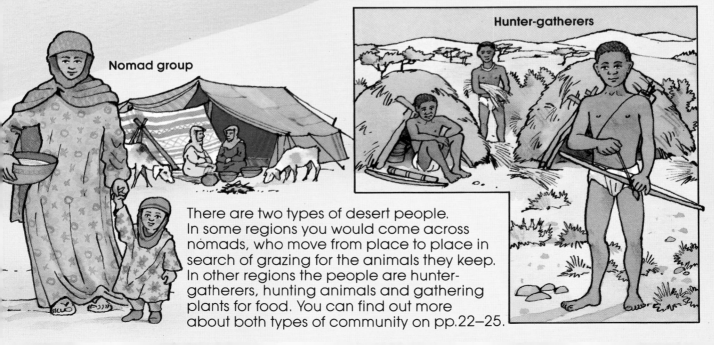

Nomad group

Hunter-gatherers

There are two types of desert people. In some regions you would come across nomads, who move from place to place in search of grazing for the animals they keep. In other regions the people are hunter-gatherers, hunting animals and gathering plants for food. You can find out more about both types of community on pp.22–25.

DESERT EXPLORERS

If you visit a desert you should not make the mistake of thinking you are the first person ever to go there. It's likely that previous visitors have been before, and their experiences might be very useful to you on your expedition. You should read their accounts and talk to local people, who have probably done some exploring themselves without writing it down. Some of the most remarkable desert journeys are shown below.

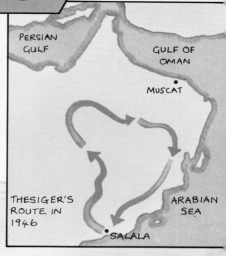

PERSIAN GULF

GULF OF OMAN

MUSCAT

THESIGER'S ROUTE IN 1946

ARABIAN SEA

SALALA

Arabia has the most difficult desert country in the World, and the 'Empty Quarter', between the Persian Gulf and the Arabian Sea, is the most barren area of all, a sea of sand with huge dunes up to 240m high.

Wilfred Thesiger made the first European crossing of the eastern part in 1946, along with four Bedu companions. They journeyed by camel over 640km of unmapped desert.

The first Australian settlers to venture into the Outback were nineteenth-century explorers, in search of fabled lakes, gold and grazing land.

In 1844 a group led by Captain Charles Sturt set out from Adelaide to look for a lake thought to be in the centre of the continent. They took bullocks, 200 sheep and even a boat.

Thesiger's main barrier was the Uruq Al Shaiba, a huge wall of sand. Al Auf, the expedition's head guide, managed to find a way through, and finally the expedition reached the oasis of Dhafar to complete their epic journey. If any of their camels had died, or if their water supply had run out, the expedition members would certainly have died.

SIMPSON DESERT

ADELAIDE

The Sahara is an immense size, and difficult to cross on foot or by camel. Arab traders have been doing it for centuries, but one of the first outsiders to make the attempt was the British Captain George Lyon, who crossed the Sahara from Egypt in 1819. He very nearly died from disease and lack of water on his journey.

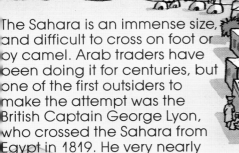

Many Arab traders used to travel across the desert from the mysterious city of Timbuktu. Until 1828 no outsider had been there, and it was rumoured to be a very wealthy place. Frenchman René Caille set out to find it, disguised as an Arab (otherwise it's likely he would have been killed). He reached the town from Senegal, and then crossed the Sahara to tell the World that Timbuktu was really only a poor settlement, built of mud bricks.

During Sturt's journey the second-in-command died and the Captain was very ill. But despite this the expedition crossed a desert which they named after Sturt, and they reached the southern edge of the Simpson Desert before they had to turn back.

In 1860 large rewards were offered to the first person who could cross Australia from South to North. A group led by Robert Burke succeeded first, but only one man survived their journey.

A group led by John Stuart also crossed the continent. His expedition survived; but Stuart himself was half-blind by the time his party staggered into Adelaide.

In 1850 the German explorer Heinrich Barth did an amazing 16,000km trip across the Sahara. His companions died on the journey, but Barth continued to Timbuktu and Lake Chad. He made valuable drawings of the plants and animals he found on the way.

The first desert explorers were very brave, but they made many mistakes which cost some of them their lives. With the right equipment and planning no-one need risk their lives on desert journeys today.

EQUIPMENT LIST

Deserts are dangerous places, and it is vital to take the right equipment on an expedition. It could save your life!

In order to travel to desert countries you need a passport and certificates to show that you have been vaccinated against diseases such as yellow fever.

You need to take rucksacks for your equipment and pack everything inside plastic bags to keep out dust and sand.

If you take a camera and film you must keep them as cool as you can. If you are camping in the same place for a while you could bury them to keep them as cold as possible.

You must take radio equipment to keep in regular contact with people who could rescue you in an emergency.

You must take a snakebite kit, including instruments to remove the poison in case you get bitten. However, it's best to get medical help first, and only use your kit as a last resort. Never try to suck the poison out — it could kill you!

You will need a compass and some satellite pictures or aerial photos as well as maps. The photos will tell you much more than the maps, which might well be out-of-date.

It would be helpful to future desert travellers if you made your own maps and wrote notes about the areas you travel through.

In the desert, sand and rocks reflect back the Sun's rays during the day, increasing the sweltering temperature. To keep cool and protect yourself from sunburn you need loosely-fitting cotton clothes: a long-sleeved shirt, long trousers and a wide-brimmed hat.

You must put strong sun cream on exposed skin and make sure your feet stay comfortable by wearing thick cotton socks and lightweight protective trekking boots.

If you are travelling by car or Land Rover you must be careful not to get stuck in soft sand. If you do, you will have to dig your way out, using boards to help the vehicle's wheels get a grip.

Alternatively you could travel by camel, but if you hire them you should hire their drivers with them, because camels can be very difficult to handle.

Water is the most important thing you need in the desert; without it you would not survive. You are likely to need at least nine litres a day, and you can never rely on water marked on a map; it may be contaminated or dried up.

You have to carry your supply with you in plastic bottles, checking them daily to make sure you have enough for your journey. You can find out about ways of finding water in the desert on p.10.

Deserts can be very cold at night, sometimes going below freezing point, so you need a good-quality sleeping bag to keep you warm. You could either use a tent or sleep outside, but it would be better to avoid sleeping on the ground if possible, in case a snake or a scorpion crawls in with you to keep itself warm! A hammock is useful if there are any trees, or you could use a camp bed to keep you off the ground.

It is a good idea to pack a metal mirror (rather than breakable glass) as a last-ditch means of contacting rescuers.

If you hold the mirror towards the Sun and move it around, it will flash brightly. Because the desert air is normally still and calm, and the landscape is often flat and bare, the light signal will be visible for many kilometres around.

DESERT SURVIVAL

To survive in the desert you must study and plan for the dangers you might encounter. Here are some common expedition problems and travel rules.

There is one rule above all others in the desert: always know where your next drink of water is coming from. You should always carry enough water to last until you reach your next known supply, and you must check your water containers regularly. Remember, you can never rely on water sources marked on maps.

If you run out of water supplies you must try to conserve the water in your body until you reach a new source. You can cut down on sweating by only travelling at night and resting in the shade during the day.

If you have some water that is unfit to drink, you could use it to wet your clothes, which helps to reduce body evaporation.

To get some emergency water you could dig a well where there might be a supply, for example where there is a dry stream bed. You could try to get a small amount by building a 'desert still', which works on the principle that even in the driest deserts there is moisture deep in the soil.

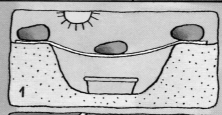

To make a still you need to dig a hole and put a bucket in the bottom. Cover the hole with polythene, sealed around the edges with rocks. When the temperature drops at night, the soil surface will get cold, but the soil down in the hole will stay warm. The polythene will get cold, and water from the soil beneath will condense on it and run into the bucket.

It *is* possible to drown in a desert! You must be careful not to sleep in dry river-beds, because rain from many kilometres away can suddenly flood down the river, turning it into a raging torrent.

You must always be careful crossing a flowing river. Beds that run through sand change depth quickly, and you may find it much deeper than you expected.

People often think it is possible to get water from desert cacti. It is true that some cacti hold water in their spongy tissue (see p.20), but it is difficult to extract, and can taste very unpleasant.

In the Kalahari Desert of East Africa the local bushmen know where to look for plant roots called tubers, which contain water. But this supply is not enough to survive on.

If you expect rescuers to search for you there are a few rules to abide by. If you have a vehicle you must stay with it; it will be more easily seen from the air and will provide shade and some water from its cooling system.

If you cannot get radio contact you could use a mirror to signal to search parties (see p. 9). If you see an aeroplane, you should flash the mirror at the pilot and lay out rocks or clothes in recognizable shapes, such as an 'X'.

There are lots of poisonous snakes and scorpions in deserts, but if you take reasonable care you can avoid them.

Never step over a rock or fallen tree without checking that it is clear of poisonous animals, and if you collect wood for burning you must check that there is nothing hiding under it. Always remember to check the ground before you sit or lie down.

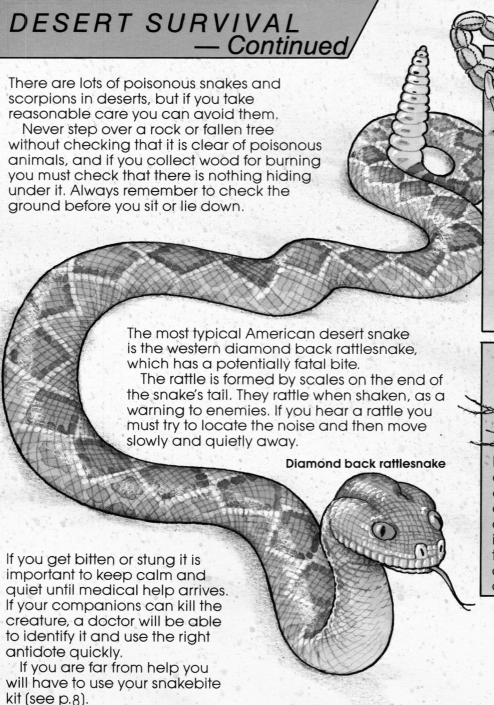

The most typical American desert snake is the western diamond back rattlesnake, which has a potentially fatal bite.

The rattle is formed by scales on the end of the snake's tail. They rattle when shaken, as a warning to enemies. If you hear a rattle you must try to locate the noise and then move slowly and quietly away.

Diamond back rattlesnake

If you get bitten or stung it is important to keep calm and quiet until medical help arrives. If your companions can kill the creature, a doctor will be able to identify it and use the right antidote quickly.

If you are far from help you will have to use your snakebite kit (see p.8).

Scorpion

All scorpions are venomous, but they are not all dangerous to humans. The venom is in the tip of the tail, and a scorpion stings by curling the tip up over its back.

Scorpions like dark corners, so you must shake out your shoes every morning, in case one has crept inside!

Mosquito

Mosquitoes, sand flies and bugs are a desert danger because they carry diseases such as malaria and sandfly fever. You need insect repellant to ward them off, and you must take anti-malaria tablets whilst on your journey.

In Africa you must be careful not to camp in places where domestic animals have been kept. Their paddocks are often marked out by bushes, laid in a circle to keep the animals in. The area may well be infested with ticks, which carry nasty diseases.

Hyena

It is unlikely that you will encounter many dangerous large animals on a desert journey, but in the Kalahari and parts of the Sahara you could find lions, leopards, and hyenas, and you should try to avoid them.

Desert travellers sometimes see mirages, caused by the hot desert air bending light rays in unusual ways.

When this happens the air shimmers and shines and looks just like a lake in the middle of the desert. It also makes distances appear much shorter than they really are.

Sometimes hot desert air can rise very quickly, whipping up sand and dust into a sandstorm.

If you see the horizon darken and an obvious haze of dust approaching, you must act quickly, closing vehicle windows and air intakes. If you are walking with a camel you must make it lie down. You should cover your own face and sit (not lie) down until the storm subsides.

When the dust cloud reaches you it will blot out the Sun, and when it has passed sand dunes may have moved or changed shape, and roads will be buried. You'll need to check your compass to decide which way to go.

Animal bodies are made up of 95% water, and without it no creature could survive. In the desert the main problem is to find a water source, but many animals have adapted to cope with the drought conditions.

There is rarely any water on the surface of a desert, and rain only falls occasionally. Animals have to get the moisture they need by eating plants or other creatures. The most well-known desert animal is the camel, which grazes on plants.

Camels are perfectly adapted for life in the desert. They can survive for many days without water (although they do not store it in their humps, as many people think). Their wide, hairy feet prevent them sinking into soft sand, and their nostrils can close up to keep out sand and dust.

Nostrils closed to keep out sand.

Foot adapted for walking on sand.

The one-humped camel, the dromedary, is a domestic working animal. The two-humped camel, the bactrian, still lives wild in the Gobi Desert of Central Asia.

There are mammals living in most deserts. An interesting example is the bighorn sheep, living in one of the hottest places on Earth, Death Valley in the Mojave Desert, USA.

In July the temperature sometimes reaches 50°C, and very few animals can survive. But the bighorn stores water in its stomach and can live off dry food for many days.

Most desert animals keep out of the sun during the day. For instance, the Arabian oryx feeds in the evening, and shelters under rocks or trees in daytime. Sometimes it scrapes a hole, so it can sit on cool sand beneath the surface of the ground.

The ground squirrel of the African Kalahari Desert uses its long bushy tail as an umbrella, holding the tail over its head to shelter it from the sun. The squirrel's feet are padded with hair to protect them from the heat of the sand.

The Saharan fennec fox spends its day in a rock crevice or a burrow, away from the heat. At night it comes out to hunt for gerbils and other small animals. It has large triangular ears which pick up sounds very well. Big ears help to keep many desert animals cool, and stop them from losing too much water through evaporation. The ears are covered with tiny blood vessels, and as air blows across them it cools the blood inside, helping to keep the animal's body temperature down.

There are many types of desert snakes and lizards. These creatures are reptiles, which means that they are cold-blooded. They cannot make their own body heat; instead they are warmed by the sun around them. When it is hot they are active, but when it is cool they have to rest.

Desert snakes eat small animals such as rodents. Rattlesnakes and asps kill their prey by biting them and injecting them with poison, whereas snakes such as African sand boas wrap their bodies round their prey and crush them.

Some desert snakes have developed a 'sidewinding' movement, to get a good grip on soft sand. They arch the front part of their bodies and throw their heads across the sand, pulling the rest of their body after them. In this way they seem to roll sideways, leaving a trail of wavering lines behind them.

Sand tracks

A sidewinding snake

The gila monster and the beaded lizard of Mexico look alike, and they are the World's only venomous lizards.

The gila monster (pronounced 'heela'), of the southern USA, can grow up to 40cm long. It eats insects and young birds, and it has a strong jaw with sharp teeth. When it bites its victim, poison trickles down grooves in its teeth into the wound.

Gila monster

The desert tortoise of North America is one of the few desert animals that stays out during the hot daytime sun.

If the tortoise gets too hot, it wets its head and neck with saliva from its mouth, and it cools its back legs with body fluid.

At night the tortoise scrapes out a hole and shelters underground.

The moloch lizard of the Australian desert has another name — the thorny devil. This is because its back is covered in spines, protecting it against attacks from predators.

The moloch feeds on black ants, sitting beside ant trails and lapping up the ants with its long tongue. It has an unusual way of getting water — it seems to be able to condense it from the air onto its skin. The water trickles down tiny grooves in the skin until it reaches the lizard's mouth.

Desert skinks are small lizards which have developed clever ways of moving underneath the surface of the sand, to protect themselves from the sun's heat.

One kind of skink, called the sandfish, lives in the Namib desert of Africa. It has no legs at all, but 'swims' through the sand, instead, hunting for beetles and millipedes.

Desert toads belong to the amphibian animal class, which means they can live on land or in water. One of the strangest desert amphibians is the spadefoot toad. It has powerful legs, which it uses for burrowing into the desert sand in its native Arizona.

During very hot spells the toad stays buried in the soil for weeks or months at a time. Its skin hardens into a waterproof coat, with just two tiny holes for breathing.

There are lots of desert insects and spiders. Few of the spiders use webs to trap their prey — there aren't many plants for them to hang webs on, and there aren't many flying insects to trap. Instead they hunt on the ground.

The red-kneed tarantula is a hunting spider which lives in the Mexican desert. Its body is thickly covered in hairs, which can pick up vibrations in the air and on the ground, telling it where prey may be found.

Tarantulas eat small reptiles, insects and other spiders.

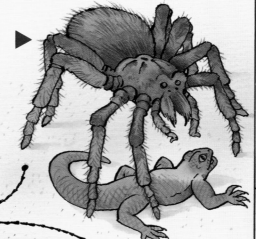

The darkling beetle of the Sahara Desert has no wings. Instead, its outer wing cases are fused together, leaving a pocket of air underneath which protects the beetle from the heat of the sun.

Tarantulas are themselves hunted by the tarantula hawk wasp, which stings and paralyses spiders and drags them to its burrow.

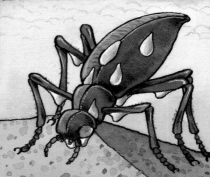

The ant lion is the larva of a fly found in the deserts of America. It catches food by digging a pit in the sand and hiding itself in the bottom.

When an ant or another insect tumbles into the pit, the ant lion seizes it with its jaws. If the victim struggles free, the ant lion throws sand at it to make it fall back into the pit.

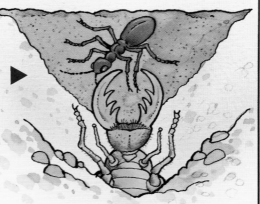

A different type of darkling beetle lives in the African Namib Desert, where clouds of fog roll in from the nearby South Atlantic Ocean. To get water the beetle stands on top of a dune. The fog condenses into water on its body and runs into its mouth.

Very few birds live in the desert. Those that *do* are usually to be found sheltering from the heat beneath any plants or rocks they can find. Their feathers are often puffed out to act as a barrier against the heat.

The ostrich is the largest bird in the World, growing to a height of up to 2.5m. It is found in parts of Africa and Australia. It eats plants, small creatures and even sand to help its digestion.

Like all desert animals, birds must get a supply of water. The African sand grouse even manages to carry water to its young. It flies to a pool and soaks up moisture in its stomach feathers. Then it returns to its nest, where its chicks suck the water from the feathers.

Ostriches are commonly thought to bury their heads in sand. In reality, an ostrich on a nest will lower its head to avoid danger, and it just *looks* as though the head has disappeared.

Roadrunners live in the deserts of Mexico and Arizona. They are famous for being fast athletes, and with their strong legs they can run at speeds of up to 37km/hr.

The roadrunner feeds mostly on snakes and lizards. It can even tackle a rattlesnake, pounding its prey with its strong bill and then swallowing the body headfirst.

19

DESERT PLANTS

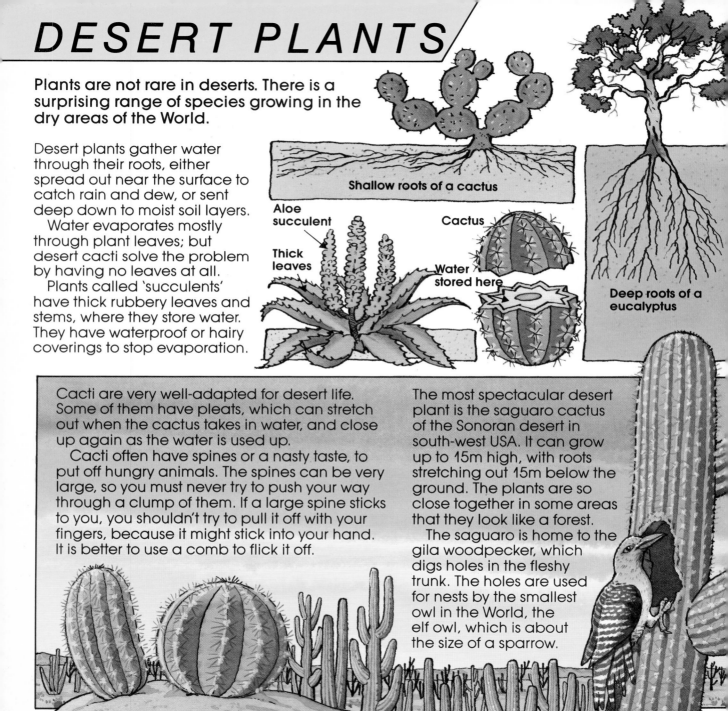

Plants are not rare in deserts. There is a surprising range of species growing in the dry areas of the World.

Desert plants gather water through their roots, either spread out near the surface to catch rain and dew, or sent deep down to moist soil layers.

Water evaporates mostly through plant leaves; but desert cacti solve the problem by having no leaves at all.

Plants called 'succulents' have thick rubbery leaves and stems, where they store water. They have waterproof or hairy coverings to stop evaporation.

Shallow roots of a cactus

Aloe succulent

Thick leaves

Cactus

Water stored here

Deep roots of a eucalyptus

Cacti are very well-adapted for desert life. Some of them have pleats, which can stretch out when the cactus takes in water, and close up again as the water is used up.

Cacti often have spines or a nasty taste, to put off hungry animals. The spines can be very large, so you must never try to push your way through a clump of them. If a large spine sticks to you, you shouldn't try to pull it off with your fingers, because it might stick into your hand. It is better to use a comb to flick it off.

The most spectacular desert plant is the saguaro cactus of the Sonoran desert in south-west USA. It can grow up to 15m high, with roots stretching out 15m below the ground. The plants are so close together in some areas that they look like a forest.

The saguaro is home to the gila woodpecker, which digs holes in the fleshy trunk. The holes are used for nests by the smallest owl in the World, the elf owl, which is about the size of a sparrow.

Mojave Desert, California, after rain.

Cacti are perennial, which means that they live for many years and survive drought seasons. But some desert plants, called 'ephemerals', avoid droughts by growing, flowering and seeding themselves only when rains come. Their seeds can then survive for many years, until the next rain falls.

Many ephemeral plants have beautiful flowers, but these only appear for a short time, after rain has fallen. They don't live very long, so they must attract pollinating insects quickly. That is why they are so brightly coloured.

There are many types of desert tree. The biggest is the baobab or bottle tree, found in the Kalahari and Australia on the edge of desert land. It has a large hollow trunk, which can grow up to 10m in diameter and store up to 1,000 litres of water. You could get emergency water supplies by splitting open the tree trunk.

Baobab tree

Many desert people are nomads, living in small family groups and moving from place to place in search of food. They often have livestock such as goats, which graze on any plants they come across.

There are several different Saharan tribes. One example are the tall Tuarag nomads, from Mali and Niger.

The Tuarag breed camels, and lead them in groups called 'caravans' across the Sahara, carrying goods such as cloth, dates and bronze ingots to Timbuktu and Bamba.

The men wear long blue robes, and on their heads they have turbans, with a long cloth which can be pulled over the nose and mouth to keep out sand.

Tuarag tents are portable and are usually made from leather, with wooden frames carved with simple decorations. A gap around the bottom of the tent allows air to circulate, and sticks are sometimes stuck around the outside to protect the tent from large animals.

If you visited the Tuarag you would probably be offered tea to drink. The brewing is a careful ceremony: the hot green tea, mixed with sugar and mint, is poured back and forth between two pots until it tastes just right. Everyone is expected to have three cupfuls and to refuse is thought rude.

The Bedouin people of the Arabian Desert live in a similar way to the Tuarag. They have the same religion — Islam — and travel the desert with their camels, sheep and goats.

A Bedouin tent is made from woollen strips of camel or goat hair sewn together. It is held up by tall poles in the middle and short poles at the sides.

The side flaps of the tent can be tied down to keep out dust and the glare of the sun, or they can be tied back to allow in a cooling breeze.

There is no furniture inside a Bedouin tent. Instead, the occupants sit on cushions and rugs they have woven.

In one corner of the tent there is usually a charcoal fire burning in a hollow in the ground. The tent may be divided into rooms by woven flaps hanging from the roof.

Many of today's Bedouin tribespeople are now selling their camels and buying motor trucks instead. They can use them to carry sheep and goats more quickly to new pastures, and it is much easier and quicker for them to drive their animals across the desert to local markets.

23

The bushmen of the African Kalahari desert do not keep animals or grow crops. They live off food they find in the desert, gathering plants and hunting animals.

Bushmen's huts are made with local materials. They have strong branches as a framework and a thatch of long grass.

Just outside their huts the bushmen usually light fires using a firestick. They place its pointed end into a notch cut in another stick, and spin it between their hands. After a while, the wood dust catches fire and falls onto a wad of dry grass. Then dry sticks are piled on top.

The bushmen are expert trackers and hunters. They use arrows and spears to kill animals in the same way as cavemen did in prehistoric times. They make the animal skins into clothing.

The bushmen find the water they need at tiny 'sipwells' in the desert, places where water has collected. They suck it up through hollow sticks and transfer it to ostrich eggshells for storage.

The women of a village spend their day collecting plant food. When water is scarce they search for tuber roots (see p.13). They scrape the tubers into a pulp and squeeze the liquid out.

The Aborigines have lived in Outback Australia for more than 40,000 years. Much of their land has been taken by settlers, but there are still a few tribes living in the old way.

The Aborigines are very practical people. They build their shelters from poles and eucalyptus bark and they weave belts, fishing lines and baskets out of string made from a bark fibre.

The Aborigines do not wander aimlessly in the desert. Each group follows a path taken by their ancestors long ago in the 'Dreamtime', a legendary period when the World began. The Aborigines believe that the people of Dreamtime were changed into rocks, plants or animals.

The Aborigines are able to live in the harsh desert by trekking in search of animals and water. They know where and when food can be found, and they are expert trackers, hunting animals such as kangaroos, emus and wombats.

When there is no big game to be found the Aborigines catch lizards, frogs and mice to eat, or they dig in the ground for ants or grubs. The ants taste rather like honey, and the grubs taste of nuts.

DESERT MYSTERIES

There are many natural desert puzzles worth solving, such as how animals adapt to desert life and how plants can survive for years with no water. There are also some dramatic and strange unexplained mysteries which you might be lucky enough to come across, and perhaps even solve, on a desert journey.

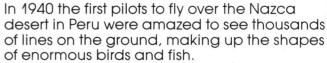

In 1876 the German explorer Erwin von Bary found crocodile tracks in the middle of the Sahara, one of the driest areas of the World. For a long time no-one believed him, until one was shot in 1908.

There are still thought to be isolated crocodile groups living in small pools in the heart of the Sahara, although no-one knows how they got there!

In 1940 the first pilots to fly over the Nazca desert in Peru were amazed to see thousands of lines on the ground, making up the shapes of enormous birds and fish.

No-one knows who made these figures or why. Some people think they are a giant calendar or a religious monument. They were drawn with great effort by clearing the top layer of desert stones away to expose the soil beneath.

In the late 1800s a German called Jacob Waltz disappeared into the Superstition mountains of the Arizona desert and returned with lots of gold. He repeated his trip many times, and reputedly found $200,000 worth of treasure.

Waltz died in Phoenix without ever revealing the location of his mine, and many people have searched for it since. No one has ever found it, but several people have died in attempts to discover the secret.

One of the commonest desert mysteries is how news travels so rapidly. For instance, you might be sitting in a tent alone in the Kalahari when suddenly a bushman will appear, having walked several kilometres to meet you.

If you asked your visitor how he knew you were there, he would probably say that he had heard, even though you may not have seen or spoken to anyone for many days. How does it happen? Some people think it is telepathy but no-one really knows.

On the arid Tassili plateau, in the Sahara, there are some beautiful rock paintings which show that the desert was once rich with animals and plants. There are pictures of antelopes, giraffe, sheep and even elephants.

Very little is known about the people who painted these mysterious pictures, but they certainly lived in a very different Sahara from the one we see today. No-one knows why the pictures were painted or how they have survived the wind and sun for so long.

DESERT FUTURE

The deserts of the World are changing quickly. Increasingly they are being developed by humans; but this can bring great dangers if it is not planned properly. Lots of careful scientific study needs to be done to prevent damage.

Food crops can be grown in desert regions if the ground is irrigated, which means it is supplied with water through man-made pipe systems and channels.

There are many new schemes for desert irrigation around the World, but they all need careful planning, or they could destroy desert soil instead of improving it and cause irreparable damage.

Deserts are being examined to see whether they can produce useful products without irrigation. For instance, native plants are being analysed to see whether any of them can produce chemicals or cattle food.

Already one desert plant, the jojoba bush, has been cultivated to produce oil which can be used for many purposes, for instance in cosmetics and hair shampoo.

If the desert people could cultivate their plants for profit they might be able to get better food supplies and a higher standard of living. Unless scientists can help them do this, many will move away from the desert to cities, and their ancient cultures could die out.

Jojoba bush

In some desert areas plant life is being destroyed, as animals over-graze the land. Eventually the soil itself is eroded by wind and rain, and land bordering the over-grazed desert is overwhelmed by wind-blown sand.

This problem is called desertification. Combined with bad farming and drought, it has resulted in the loss of millions of hectares of farmland.

The deserts formed in this way are barren and ugly. One example is the Sahel region, south of the Sahara. A few years ago a drought dried up the soil, killed the plants and has resulted in the Sahara spreading south by many kilometres. Scientists are trying to slow down the desertification process.

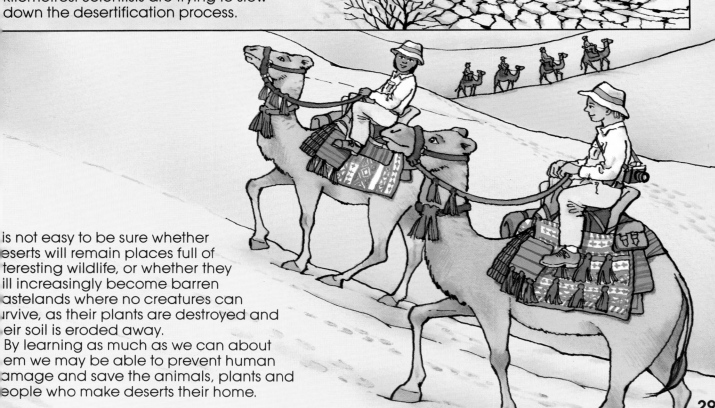

is not easy to be sure whether eserts will remain places full of teresting wildlife, or whether they ill increasingly become barren astelands where no creatures can urvive, as their plants are destroyed and eir soil is eroded away.

By learning as much as we can about em we may be able to prevent human amage and save the animals, plants and eople who make deserts their home.

INDEX

If you would like to know more about desert people you can contact the address shown below:

Survival International,
310 Edgware Road,
London W2 1DY
Tel: 01-723 5535